To Hawa,
Best Regards !
From Arthur Ziffer

3/20/14

COUNTERTRANSFERENCE
AND
RETRIBUTION

COUNTERTRANSFERENCE
AND
RETRIBUTION

Two Plays

by

Arthur Ziffer

Library of Congress Control Number:		2012909632
ISBN:	Hardcover	978-1-4797-1145-1
	Softcover	978-1-4535-7873-5
	Ebook	978-1-4535-7874-2

This book was printed in the United States of America.

To order additional copies of this book, contact:
Xlibris Corporation
1-888-795-4274
www.Xlibris.com
Orders@Xlibris.com
87224

Table of Contents

COUNTERTRANSFERENCE

A One Act Play

Characters

Patient

Therapist

At rise:
A therapist and a patient are having a discussion in the therapist's office.

Therapist

From your phone call, I get the impression that you want to complain about a previous therapy, or to be precise, a psychotherapy, and, more specifically, a therapy with the designation "talk therapy," like psychoanalysis.

Patient

Actually, I want to complain about three or four of them, and also complain about some talk therapists that I only saw once.

Therapist

Before you go on, I'd like you to know, that as far as I am concerned, many talk therapists can be ineffective and, unfortunately, can sometimes even do harm to patients. There are some good ones but you probably couldn't afford one of them. I like to think of myself as one of the good ones. You're here because I like to help people like you, who seemed to have had a difficult time in therapy. In fact, this is my mission in life.

Patient

Thank you, I like what you say, and am I glad that I came here, at least so far.

Therapist

You're right. I could turn out to be as ineffective as your previous therapists.

Patient

To be honest, my last therapist was okay. He was a contracts lawyer who had gotten a Master's degree in psychoanalysis. I left him because it seemed like it might have been too late in my life for him to do me any good.

Therapist

Let's hope I can do better than that.

Patient

I hope so.

Therapist

The first thing we should discuss is your complicity in your bad experiences with therapy. To start with, tell me why you started going to a therapist.

Patient

This is embarrassing. I have a sexual problem. I am essentially non-orgastic.

Therapist

Is that what made you go to a therapist?

Patient

Yes, and for some other reasons also. But to get right to the point, the therapy didn't seem to work too well because of what I learned is called countertransference on the part of the therapist.

Therapist

Can you give me the details?

Patient

After a few years of preliminary, there was an incident with a woman, who worked at the same place that I did, who seemed, at least in my mind, to give me an invitation. Whereupon I froze up and did nothing. I reported the incident in therapy when it happened. The therapist said nothing at that time. A few days later—I was going four times a week—I started bemoaning about my freezing up and wondering why I had done that. The therapist made a point of saying that nothing had happened and that therefore no freeze up had occurred. This meant to me that he, subconsciously, felt guilty about letting me miss an opportunity without forcing me to focus on it. This then became the focal point of the therapy from then on: me trying to get him to admit he made a mistake and him denying it. This period seemed to be characterized by a session in which I asked him, if he had subconsciously wanted to encourage me to respond when I told him about the incident at work; and, that subconsciously he was feeling guilty about not doing so. His reply was that he didn't answer "iffy" questions. The word "iffy" galled me no end. It seemed, in retrospect, as if I was asking him for permission to go after women and he was refusing to give it to me. This period lasted for a long time and seemed to highlight the morass of countertransference that there was between me and the therapist and might have fixed in my mind the fact that I did not have his permission (the disapproving father in the oedipal triangle) to get a woman.

Therapist

Do you feel any complicity in what happened with the therapist?

Patient

Yes, in this situation and one other where this time I was being made angry by a boss of mine: I, instead of expressing my anger, just complained to some friends. In both cases the friend, different in each situation, got annoyed with me. This indicated to me that instead of complaining, I should have been expressing my displeasure to the appropriate person—my therapist or the provocative boss. Also, a lot of women have indicated to me that I was too "goody-goody," that is to say that I seemed too non-assertive.

If the woman was nice, she would tell me that I seemed like a clergyman; if she was not so nice, she would indicate to me that she didn't think I was aggressive enough in getting my fair share of sex.

Therapist

Okay I hear that, but did your therapist ever admit that he might have made a mistake?

Patient

Yes, after much time had passed and I had become very annoyed, he said, referring to the "freeze" incident, "Is there no atonement?"

Therapist

What was your response?

Patient

I said, because I was so annoyed, that I wasn't interested in atonement, but rather I wanted the incident undone.

Therapist

What did he say to that?

Patient

He said, "Atonement for a mistake includes the mistake being undone."

Therapist

And what did you say then?

Patient

I said, still vey annoyed, "No it doesn't, atonement for a mistake just means to make up for the mistake, but not the undoing of it."

Therapist

You were being very hard on him.

Patient

Yes, but what he offered was too little too late. Besides, "atonement" is sort of a vapid word.

Therapist

What was his reaction to this?

Patient

We started arguing about the meaning of the word "atonement." He felt that, as a psychiatrist, he was more of an expert on words than I was.

Therapist

You disagreed.

Patient

Yes, I said, a mathematician, which is what I am, is more likely to be an expert on words, and especially their meanings, than a psychiatrist.

Therapist

What was the upshot of this?

Patient

It became part of the countertransference morass for a few weeks or even possibly longer.

Therapist

Did it occur to you to go to another therapist for a consultation during this period?

Patient

I did.

Therapist

What happened?

Patient

As soon as I mentioned the word "countertransference," the other therapist started making fun of me, and saying in an insulting manner things like, did I think of my therapist as an older brother? Whereupon I asked him if it was appropriate for him to be talking to me like he was, and he said, in an aggressive voice, something like, "Why not, we were never going to see each other again." And that is what happened. I should have gotten up and walked out then, but as is my wont to be slow on the trigger, I stayed for the full hour (50 minutes).

Therapist

I guess he felt threatened by your bringing up the word "countertransference."

Patient

Speaking about feeling threatened by certain words, the few times I went to sex therapists, they would get angry if I mentioned the word "orgasm."

Therapist

Yes, I feel that most sex therapists are non-orgastic and would be upset by the word "orgasm."

Patient

That's interesting. I guess I agree with that.

Therapist

Tell me about your experiences with sex therapists; I have always found that they are the bottom of the barrel in the barrel of therapists.

Patient

Yes, I went to one who said, after I mentioned the word "orgasm" and that I had read Wilhelm Reich, "Well you seem to know all the words and have read all the books, but I don't know why I am here with you when I could be home with my wife and kids." I felt like saying, "I can't believe that you have been licensed to inflict yourself on the public."

Therapist

You should have; or, maybe said, "Well why aren't you at home with your wife and kids?" Are there any other experiences with sex therapists that you'd like to tell me about?

Patient

I went to one who ended the session at half a session because I annoyed her by showing up early and also for, probably, using the word "orgasm." She told me she only saw couples and to go see somebody, who it turned out I had already seen and who was really bad news. He wanted me to have a sexual relationship with anybody I could without worrying about having the right feelings toward the person. When I said that that might have gotten me into trouble in the past, he said, "That was then; this is now." I found that very annoying. He also talked about me to another patient who worked at the same place I did. He told my co-worker that he had had to dismiss me from the therapy, which wasn't true, although in this case I wouldn't have cared if he had.

Therapist

To get back to your first therapy, did you ever confront your therapist with the fact that he was possibly indulging in countertransference?

Patient

I did once suggest that during our seemingly never ending morass of countertransference that maybe he should check out our situation out with somebody else, like another therapist.

Therapist

How did he react?

Patient

As I remember he said nothing.

Therapist

Do you have any idea why you and he had a problem?

Patient

Not to blame everything on non-orgasticity, although Wilhelm Reich seemed to, I guess he was non-orgastic and/or maybe he felt threatened by me.

Therapist

Why do say that?

Patient

At one session, I don't remember what brought it up, he said to me, "Haven't you ever been 'all fucked-out'?" The use of those words indicated to me that he was either non-orgastic or he felt threatened by me.

Therapist

I agree; those words would certainly have bothered me. But before we go on, did you have any clue early into the therapy that you were going to have problems with your therapist.

Patient

Yes, right from the start.

Therapist

How so?

Patient

Before going to the therapist, I read Karen Horney's book "Are You Considering Psychoanalysis?" In it she says, that the patient should ask the therapist, what are the goals that the therapist has for the patient to reach in therapy?

Therapist

Yes, I read the book and remember that. So what happened?

Patient

The therapist refused to answer the question directly; probably asking me in a flip way, which, by the way, happened many times, "Why do you ask?"

Therapist

I guess you feel that you should have quit right then.

Patient

Yes, but I was desperate and I decided to ignore it.

Therapist

That's understandable. But, to jump a few years ahead, and get back to the way your first therapy did end, did your therapist try to stop you from ending at that time?

Patient

Sort of, but I thought that the therapist always tries to stop the patient from ending therapy to make sure that the patient should really quit.

Therapist

But what about the reasons, namely your sexual difficulties, that you went to the therapist for in the first place?

Patient

Those reasons seem to pale when you get into the grinding morass of a therapy racked by countertransference. It seems that therapy just becomes an endless routine of the therapist whipping the patient with remarks like "Why do you ask?", "What do you think?", or "What's it all about?" After a while there seems to be nothing left to do but find some way to end it.

Therapist

What was the manner of the therapist when you ended?

Patient

It seemed that he was smirking, making me feel that I had let him cheat me out of five years of my life, a lot of money, and that he had beaten me in a will conflict.

Therapist

How did that ending work out?

Patient

It was a disaster. Firstly, because I needed an excuse to quit therapy, I quit a great work situation, which never came up again. Secondly, after several months, I realized how angry I was at the therapist. I used to curse and holler when I was by myself in my car and apartment. In fact, once I went out with a woman that lived on my floor in my apartment building and after telling her that I was having some difficult therapeutic reactions like cursing and hollering by myself in my apartment, I asked her if anybody could hear me. She said, "Yes" and that I was known as the man that screamed in the night. I then decided I had to go back to the therapist and curse and holler at him.

Therapist

Did he let you come back?

Patient

Yes, lucky for me, he did.

Therapist

What happened?

Patient

I began to express my anger. At first I was restrained. But as time went by, I got to be more and more forceful. Finally, I reached the point, in one session, where I was as expressive in his office as I was when cursing and hollering by myself.

Therapist

How did that work out?

Patient

At that particular session he said that if I was going to keep this up we had to end.

Therapist

And how did you react?

Patient

Amazingly to myself, I said okay, and then I unilaterally picked an ending date, two or so weeks from then. I guess I felt that if he said that to me there was no point in my coming to him anymore. I felt that by threatening me with the end of therapy, he was missing the point of my cursing and hollering at him. Also I had reached the point where I would not have to curse and holler by myself. The latter meaning that I had resolved, what can be called, the "anger debt" that I had built up, that were, hopefully, the result of the therapist's misdeeds and not mine.

Therapist

What did the therapist say?

Patient

He said nothing.

Therapist

What happened in the next few days?

Patient

We never discussed the upcoming ending. However, at one point, I did say that I felt like killing him. I guess I had decided that by his precipitating the end of the therapy, as I felt he did, that he had proved to me that countertransference had been operating and that maybe I had wasted a lot of years.

Therapist

How did he react to that?

Patient

He said he was prepared to defend himself.

Therapist

Wow! What happened on the supposed last day?

Patient

After my bringing up that the present day was our last day, he said, "I was only kidding." Whereupon I said, "You weren't kidding but were trying to bluff me into being quiet."

Therapist

And what did he say then?

Patient

He said nothing then but at the end of the session, he said, "Please come one more time."

Therapist

What did you do?

Patient

I came, thinking that if we did end when I said we would end, he was cheating me out of an appropriate ending and/or maybe I was hoping he would say something like—now that I finally had expressed my anger appropriately and called his bluff—we can really begin therapy.

Therapist

I guess he didn't say that, but what did he say?

Patient

There were tears in his eyes, his face was very white, and he said in a whiney voice, "If I wanted to quit that was okay but he would keep a few sessions open in case I changed my mind."

Therapist

As far as I am concerned this ending proves that countertransference was operating as you thought. Do you think that before coming to that last session he tried to check out with another colleague what was happening and what he should do?

Patient

I don't know; there wasn't a lot of time for him to do that between the session he asked me to come one more time (which turned out to be our next to last session) and the actual last session.

Therapist

Did you ever go back?

Patient

Not then, but eleven or twelve years later I had to go back to him to get his signature for permission to take flying lessons.

Therapist

What happened then?

Patient

He signed the form for me to take the flying lessons and then asked me how I was doing with the ladies. When I indicated that I wasn't doing very well, he seemed very upset.

Therapist

What did that mean to you?

Patient

That, in retrospect, he had realized what a shambles he had made of my therapy and possibly had exacerbated my oedipal problems with women by playing, over and over again, the role of the disapproving father figure with the endless hassling that we had had over the woman that I had froze up on. This might have crystallized into something that has plagued me ever since then; namely, when I meet a woman who appeals to me I seem to have trouble going after her; I hesitate. And, furthermore, this is combined with the fact that if I do get myself to go after the woman, I don't seem to be too upset if she rejects me. In fact, sometimes I am even relieved that I made the approach but didn't have to get involved. It seems that women who appeal to me have become, to coin a term, a "no-no."

Therapist

You know that to a lot of people the notion of women being a "no-no" will bring up the issue of whether or not you are gay.

Patient

I am not gay. By the way, does a person have to be either straight or gay?

Therapist

Good reply. Let's go on. It seems that there are two ways of looking at your therapy. The first is that you seemed like such a victim type personality to your therapist that, subconsciously, he decided to abuse you until you fought back, like little kids picking on a weakling in the schoolyard until he fights back, if he ever does. The second is that you were in a classic case of countertransference and did the only thing you could do to extricate yourself from the therapy; otherwise, you would have found yourself in what Freud called "Analysis Terminable and Interminable". As I said before, I favor the latter explanation. Of course, it could have been a combination of both, but mostly the second.

Patient

Actually, I got validation that it was the second one.

Therapist

Can you explain that?

Patient

One day, I met somebody, who had taken a trigonometry course from me years before; and, upon finding out that he had become a psychiatrist, I told him the sad story about my own therapy. When I finished, he asked me the name of my therapist. After I told him, he then told me that in his psychiatric residency, he had had a run-in with my therapist, who was on staff at the same hospital where he was doing his residency; and, he had to finish his residency elsewhere. He said my therapist was the kind of person who was overbearing and could never admit that he had made a mistake.

Therapist

That certainly was validation but it hasn't seemed to help you with women.

Patient

No, but was my therapy my main problem with women? It did seem that whenever I met a woman I could be interested in, while I was still in therapy, I would hesitate thinking that I had to prove myself by ending the miasma of therapy before I could go after her, like a young soldier who has to prove himself in battle before he feels ready to take on the responsibility of a wife and family. Furthermore, as I indicated before, it seemed that I had developed a bad habit of hesitation with women that I liked, even after the therapy ended. Could I blame this permanent hesitation reaction only on the therapy or was there something else operating?

Therapist

It's hard to say.

Patient

By the way, did I let the therapist off too easy? Should I have come back when he said he would keep some hours open for me and continued expressing my anger with the same force, that is to say, to coin another term, to "blast" him, like I did in the session that precipitated the ending?

Therapist

That's a good question. Pardon me if I ask, a la your therapist, what do you think?

Patient

I guess I figured that I had shown, at least to myself, that the therapist had no idea what had been happening during the therapy and that it was time to leave. Also, I had done one of the things one needs to do to end a therapy, and that is I had freed myself of him by blasting him. One of the big problems with therapy, after you get into it and decide it is not going anywhere, is how to end it without feeling the urge to go back if one has built up an "anger debt" and not resolved it during the therapy. Of course this assumes that an anger debt is justifiable and not just negative transference. When I first contemplated going to therapy, people who had

had experience with therapy, warned me about the problem of ending therapy, and I said, well I could always just quit. Little did I know?

Therapist

After you left therapy, how do you think your therapist felt?

Patient

As I said before, from his reaction when I went back eleven or twelve years later to get him to approve my taking flying lessons, I got the impression he felt guilty about screwing up my therapy.

Therapist

Do you think he changed as a therapist?

Patient

Yes, from something he said, I got the impression that he became much more tolerant of patients getting loud.

Therapist

So his experience with you might have made him a better therapist.

Patient

Yes.

Therapist

Do you forgive him?

Patient

No, my therapist should have gone to another therapist and discussed my case which would have made him realize that countertransference had reared its ugly head.

Therapist

Have you ever hurt anybody seriously?

Patient

Yes.

Therapist

Tell me about this.

Patient

There was a woman who liked me, who I sort of rejected cruelly (by being thoughtless); it caused her to quit her job and she has never gotten back on her feet work-wise. Also, there were many other women I hurt, some by rejection, and some by just not responding to them when they indicated that they liked me. I seem to be very insensitive to women's feelings and men's too if the truth be told.

Therapist

So maybe you are no better than your therapist.

Patient

I didn't realize how much I was hurting those women. Of course, it could be that I just wanted, unconsciously, to hurt women, maybe to get even with them for the fact that my mother was less than perfect. But if my therapist had been better at his job and help me discover why I wanted to get even with women, then maybe I wouldn't have been such a disaster in human relationships.

Therapist

Okay. Let's go on, did you have similar problems with your other therapies?

Patient

Yes, about ten years after the first therapy ended, I decided to go to group therapy with an MD psychiatrist as group leader, thinking that if the leader was screwing up, then the other patients might come to my aid.

Therapist

How did that work out?

Patient

Not so good. Whenever the therapist would step out of line, nobody would come to my aid. It seemed the group's members were created in the therapist's image or were too passive too help me. He did, however, when some woman at work, a different one than the "freeze" woman, who became bitchy to me and turned me on, say encouragingly, "Go for cure." For various reasons I wasn't able to bring myself to respond to that push, but I wish I had.

Therapist

Can you give me an example of the group leader stepping out of line?

Patient

Yes. There was a woman in the group who, in my opinion, once she decided that I wasn't interested in her, would start picking up and brandishing a heavy ashtray and threatening to throw it at me, saying this was in case I attacked her, which of course I was not planning to do. I asked the group leader, who besides running the group had individual sessions with the group members, about this during an individual session; and, he said, unbelievably, she would probably miss me if she threw it at me. So I said that he should prove this to me by having her throw it at him. That was the end of my individual sessions with him, although I still continued group sessions for a while.

Therapist

Good for you, but how did the group end?

Patient

Again, I quit inappropriately a first time, namely, apologetically, and had to go back and quit appropriately by blasting my way out to resolve the so-called anger debt. Hopefully, the anger debt was based on unrequited abuse I had received from group members and not my own negative transference. The group leader did try to keep me in the group by indicating that I had learned how to express justifiable anger and now it was time to learn how to deal with positive feelings.

Therapist

Interesting, and slightly redeeming for him. Were there any other therapeutic mishaps?

Patient

Yes. I decided since my first two therapists were MD psychiatrists, I should go to a PhD clinical psychologist. I guess you've heard the story that when a child of an MD who was not a psychiatrist told the MD that they wanted to go to a psychiatrist, the MD said, "Don't go to a psychiatrist, I know what they are like," meaning that psychiatrists were probably riddled with their own problems and could not be effective (because of countertransference) in helping patients.

Therapist

Yes, I have heard the story. How did going to a PhD clinical psychologist work out?

Patient

Before I tell you, I should ask if the Hippocratic Oath applies to MDs that do talk therapy.

Therapist

I know where you're going with this: you're going to bring up the notion of the Hippocratic Oath becoming the hypocrite's oath. Let's not go there and get back to the PhD clinical psychologist.

Patient

After I stopped individual sessions with the group leader, I went to one to get help with my problems in group therapy. But he said I should just quit group and go to him. I said I couldn't just quit group; I felt that I had built up too much of an anger debt there. He then said that, notwithstanding the anger debt, I should just quit the group and everything would work out. Whereupon, without realizing it, I put him to the test: I did something that made him angry (to see how he would behave); instead of proving to me there was another way of resolving anger, he blasted me; so (the next session) I blasted back and he ended the therapy right then. He did, however, call me up a month later to see, presumably, if I wanted to come back. I told him that I felt that the only way to deal with the group, which is why I went to him in the first place, was to blast out. This happened when one day somebody showed up new to the group who seemed relatively supportive. I took advantage of this by blasting then and ending it as I said before.

Therapist

It seemed that you were safer in a group with other people there to keep the therapist honest than in your individual therapies, even though one was with an MD and the other with a PhD. So you were right about group putting a check on therapeutic misbehavior. But in all these supposed countertransference situations, did you worry about how much of what you thought was countertransference was really transference? You already have brought this up, but let's focus on it.

Patient

Of course, as I think I have already indicated, but I decided to trust myself. Besides, there was too much evidence for countertransference. There was my old trigonometry student who seemed to validate me. Also my first therapist did something which I thought was a sure indication of countertransference. One day out of the blue, he announced that from then on, if I wanted to cancel an hour, I not only had to give 24 hours notice, which was the old rule, but that he had to be able to fill the hour. I said that I did not like being responsible for him filling an hour and he said it didn't matter whether I liked it or not that was the way it was going to be.

Therapist

How did you respond to that?

Patient

I said that in that case, I would never tell him if I had to cancel an hour, but would pay for it. I decided not to go to the next session because I was angry at him for what I felt was an example of countertransference and he called me up to come to the session. You'd think he would have realized how countertransferential that call was, at least in my opinion.

Therapist

Good for you and yes, what he did was very countertransferential.

Patient

Also, to really expose, at least in my mind, the countertransference, I asked him one time when he and I were arguing about something and he was insisting that he was right, how did he know he was right? Whereupon he said that if he felt that he was right and thought that he was right then he was right. Then I brought up the Freudian theory of the subconscious that one could not always trust one's mind. What's that saying, the mind is a treacherous enemy. It didn't seem to register with him.

Therapist

Of course! Tell me did you have any problem with being loud when you felt aggrieved?

Patient

It seems to me that my being loud was a problem in therapy. With the first therapist it seemed that he brought up the fact that several times my loudness was complained about by other therapists who had offices near his office. The problem was that he would leave the window open instead of closing the window and using the air conditioning.

Therapist

Keeping the window open was certainly inappropriate.

Patient

Why is there such a problem with hollering at a therapist? I remember one therapist who I met socially who said to me that she would have a patient committed if a patient hollered at her.

Therapist

That's frightening. I hope therapists don't have that power and I don't think they do.

Patient

It seems that the basic rule of psychoanalysis, to free associate verbally, has to allow for free association in the appropriate tone of voice; namely, hollering when that seems necessary.

Therapist

Yes, of course; it's amazing how many therapists don't realize that. Therapists like doctors are treated like they are omniscient and after a while they can't believe they made a mistake and maybe deserve being hollered at.

Patient

So I guess we have come to the point of making a final decision on whether my problems with my therapists were countertransference or transference or a combination of both? Could it be that my early development produced in me a victim mentality where even therapists could not but help victimizing me; and, therefore my problems with the therapist were ones that could be considered as results of transference? Also, could it be that my so-called anger debts that seemed to come up in my various therapy stints were just my transferring my basic anger from unresolved childhood experiences onto the therapists, who were not the cause of my anger debts and who should not have been the recipients of my anger?

Therapist

I don't think your anger debt experiences were based on transference. Also your idea that you provoked your therapists into victimizing you, I don't agree with. Your therapists should not have indulged in the victimization process even if you were provoking it. Therefore in my opinion your problems with therapists were countertransference in all three cases. Furthermore, if you hadn't done what you did, you would probably not be alive today. Repressing anger can be very deadly: if a person doesn't realize that he has been violated, many diseases like asthma, ulcers, and also things like automobile accidents are among the possible results. Did you ever have any stomach problems or automobile accidents that had a psychological overtone?

Patient

As far as stomach problems go, after quitting the first therapist the first time, my stomach began to bother me. When I read somewhere that stomach problems can be the result of repressing anger, I said to myself, "Who am I angry at?" As soon as I asked myself that question, I realized that I was angry at my old therapist, and my stomach cleared up like magic. Of course then I went into my angry mode. In fact, one time when I was cursing and hollering to myself while driving my car (one of the few places one can do such and maybe not be noticed), a co-worker drove by and saw me doing this. The next day he came into my office a little disturbed and asked me about it. I told him that he had caught me with a case of the "screamies." He, being a savvy guy and much like me, understood what I said and walked out mollified. Also, I have had two automobile accidents that were the result of repressed anger in very obvious ways.

Therapist

The cursing and hollering seemed to work out for your benefit. It resulted in learning how not to repress anger and thereby stay alive and healthy. Also you probably helped your therapist, after you left therapy with him, to understand the process of therapy and the importance of the patients expressing anger, assuming it is justified.

Patient

You mean my therapy was less than optimal or worse so some therapist could learn his job.

Therapist

Suppose you had to choose between what happened to you in therapy or being paralyzed by a surgeon's mistake, which would you choose?

Patient

I would, of course, choose what happened in therapy rather than being paralyzed by a surgeon. But why can't a therapist learn his job before he starts working with patients and not end up hurting one or more of them? I mean shouldn't that be part of a therapist's training, that is to say, to learn how not to make a therapeutic mistake like countertransference.

Therapist

It would be nice, if therapists were effective right from the beginning of their careers (and, unfortunately, some never become effective), but it doesn't seem to work out that way.

Patient

But isn't there supposed to be a training analysis to make them competent right from the start of their practice?

Therapist

Not always, and if there is one, it is not a real therapy for several reasons: one, the trainee as a patient (with problems like most people who are interested in becoming therapists) is going to therapy before he or she has reached a dead end in life, since he or she is still in a learning phase and it's easy to stay pasted together when in that phase; two, the trainer will not certify the trainee to work as a therapist unless the trainee succumbs, in the almost necessary conflict situation that arises in any real therapy, to the interpretation of the trainer (although I wonder how much of therapeutic conflicts are based on trainer countertransference); and, thirdly, a training analysis might be for a fixed length of time which could be arbitrary and inappropriate. I don't mean to be cynical but the word "therapist" consists of the two words "the" and "rapist".

Patient
So what about me?

Therapist
You survived. Most patients would have been destroyed in the situation you were in. Haven't you ever seen a person walking along the street muttering and gesticulating to themselves? I wonder how many of them went through what you went through in therapy but without your finally blasting out to resolve the accumulated (justifiable) anger debt. Your extra resources kept you sane in the struggle, although your extra resources might have made you more provocative to the therapist and helped bring about the countertransference. Also you learned to not repress anger, which as I have said is why you might be still alive. Finally, you might have saved some patients who came to your therapist after you from having to go through what you went through because of what your therapist learned from having you as a patient.

Patient
That's all very interesting. However, I am more interested in the possibility that my first therapist might have made women a no-no for me by playing the disapproving countertransferential father in my therapeutically induced oedipal complex.

Therapist
Yes, I understand that.

Patient
Can I do anything about that?

Therapist

I am hoping that now that you fully realize what your first therapist did to you, you can overcome this problem of women being a no-no and do it without having to go for any more therapy.

Patient

I hope so. But now I think we should deal with the issue of whether we can call countertransference malpractice.

Therapist

In your case, I would call the countertransference situations you endured as malpractice. The trouble is that with talk therapy with an MD, unlike other branches of medicine, you probably would not have been able to prove malpractice.

Patient

Yes, I once asked a malpractice lawyer about my case. She said that in order to prove malpractice I would have to prove that my life had been made worse by my going to a therapist.

Therapist

That would have been difficult.

Patient

To avoid countertransference, do you have any ideas about how to eliminate it or at least reduce its occurrence?

Therapist

One way would be to make it mandatory that therapists no matter how experienced they are have to periodically discuss their cases with other therapists; this might bring about exposing a countertransference situation.

Patient

You said one way, are there any other possible ways?

Therapist

Another way would be to record every session and give the recordings to the patients who then if they feel if they are in a countertransference situation can go to a therapist arbitrator.

Patient

How would patients know about therapist arbitrators?

Therapist

At the beginning of every therapy, the patient would be given the information about the recordings, the therapy arbitrator, and the contact information of the arbitrator.

Patient

Wouldn't a lot of patients in the throes of negative transference be going to the therapy arbitrator complaining about countertransference?

Therapist

Yes, but the therapy arbitrator could tell the difference by listening to the recordings of sessions.

Patient

Both of those sound like good ideas.

Therapist

Of course maybe a combination of those would even be better. Furthermore, just the fact of these preventative measures might make therapists toe the line more. I doubt if your group leader would have said that your nemesis in the group would have probably missed you with the ashtray if she did throw it at you if he knew he was being recorded.

Patient

I guess so . . . Have we have reached the end of our work together?

Therapist

I think so.

Patient

Well, thank you and goodbye!

Therapist

Goodbye and good luck!

RETRIBUTION

A Two Act Play

Characters

First Detective

Second Detective

Psychiatrist

Girlfriend of Victim

Man/Defendant

Prosecutor

Defense Attorney

Psychiatrist for the State

ACT I

Scene 1

At Rise:
Girlfriend of a psychiatrist who was killed and the man who killed him are talking in girlfriend's apartment.

Girlfriend

(Hollering at man.) You killed my date. You hit him with a pipe. You killed him.

Man

Please don't scream at me.

Girlfriend

You followed me home. Why?

Man

I couldn't resist.

Girlfriend

Are you going to kill me too? I am the only witness to the killing.

Man

No.

Girlfriend

God, this is a strange conversation.

Man

Yes it is.

Girlfriend

I am not afraid of you.

Man

I am glad, because I have no intention of hurting you.

Girlfriend

So why did you follow me home.

Man

Because you are such a beautiful woman. Also I was curious why you left after you bent down and touched your date's neck? Although I guess you were seeing if he was dead.

Girlfriend

Yes, once I saw that he was dead and I could do nothing for him, I left because I didn't want to get involved.

Man

You are involved. Sooner or later the police are going to find out that you were out with him tonight.

Girlfriend

Oh my God!

Man

You touched his throat to check his pulse. Are you a medical person?

Girlfriend

I am a nurse practitioner.

Man

Is that like a physician's assistant?

Girlfriend

Sort of, similar amount of training, but a little different.

Man

You are so beautiful; I would have thought that you were a dancer.

Girlfriend

I did study ballet from the age of four till I graduated high school.

Man

Why did you become a nurse instead of a professional dancer?

Girlfriend

There are too many dancers; it is very competitive. But why are we making small talk? You have just killed somebody. You killed my date.

Man

God, I can't believe I did that.

Girlfriend

You mean you don't know why you killed him?

Man

I don't know exactly. I saw him leave the theater with you and I lost it. Were you very close?

Girlfriend

No, we just started dating.

Man

I knew him way back when and he was a jerk. What did you see in him?

Girlfriend

He was tall, good looking, and a doctor.

Man

Did you know that he thought of himself as the reincarnation of Freud? Like Freud he was a neurologist who became a psychiatrist. Only in his case the word "fraud" with an "a" not "Freud" with an "e" should be used.

Girlfriend

Very clever, but how did you know him?

Man

He was my psychiatrist for several years.

Girlfriend

And?

Man

He was not very good as a psychiatrist and hurt me very much.

Girlfriend

Does that justify killing him? There are lots of doctors who have patients who feel that their doctors were not good. That's why doctors have malpractice insurance.

Man

But this was much worse than malpractice.

Girlfriend

How much worse could it have been?

Man

He made it impossible for me to get or have a woman.

Girlfriend

You mean he castrated you.

Man

In a sense!

Girlfriend

What do you mean? He certainly didn't cut off your genitals?

Man

Not physically, but emotionally.

Girlfriend

Can you explain that?

Man

According to another psychiatrist, it seems that he did something in the therapy that built into me, or at least, intensified in me an inability to approach women, especially if they appeal to me.

Girlfriend

How could he do that?

Man

I not sure I can explain it.

Girlfriend

Try.

Man

The second psychiatrist called it "countertransference."

Girlfriend

Don't you mean transference?

Man

No, transference refers to a patient transferring feelings onto the psychiatrist. countertransference is where the psychiatrist transfers feelings onto the patient.

Girlfriend

I know that transference is very common in therapy. Is countertransference also common?

Man

It seems that it is.

Girlfriend

I've read that transference is supposed to be necessary in any effective talk therapy. Is countertransference also necessary?

Man

Not only is it not necessary, but it can be very harmful to the patient.

Girlfriend

Can you explain that?

Man

In my case, the psychiatrist and I argued over a woman for years.

Girlfriend

What! Can you explain that?

Man

There was this woman at work, who appealed to me and who seemed to give me, after much back and forth, an opening to approach her. But I froze and did nothing.

Girlfriend

So! Don't a lot of men do that?

Man

Probably, but after a few days when I realized what I had done and started bemoaning about my inability to have responded to the woman, my psychiatrist claimed she did not give me an opening and therefore I did not freeze, since there was nothing to freeze about.

Girlfriend

Could he have been right?

Man

Of course, but I still should have checked out the situation; and maybe he should have pointed out to me what I was doing.

Girlfriend

Don't some therapists feel that they should not intervene in things like that? But why would he feel that nothing had happened? He wasn't there when the incident occurred.

Man

Exactly

Girlfriend

So how does the countertransference fit in?

Man

I guess unconsciously he felt guilty about not making me aware of what I did, because of inattention or maybe he felt guilty over not wanting me getting something out of life that he never could get (Psychiatrists want the best for their patients but something better for themselves.) and that made him angry at me.

Girlfriend

From my few dates with him, I could tell that he was the kind of person that would find it difficult to admit that he had made a mistake. But how did that make it impossible for you to approach women?

Man

As a second psychiatrist explained it to me, the so-called oedipal triangle from the Oedipus complex—with the first psychiatrist being the disapproving father, the woman the mother, and me the son—was intensified no end.

Girlfriend

Isn't the Oedipus complex about a man wanting to sleep with his mother?

Man

That's an oversimplification; a man wants to sleep with a suitable substitute for the mother. I'm sure you've heard the song that begins, "I want a girl just like the girl that married dear old dad."

Girlfriend

How can you combine that hokey song with the Oedipus complex?

Man

I don't think I can explain the complications of the Oedipus complex to you.

Girlfriend

Can't a man just meet a woman and there be no other man involved?

Man

Yes, if the man has resolved the basic Freudian complication of the oedipal triangle. However, a lot of men seem to reach adulthood with an unresolved oedipal fixation which leads to various problems. One of the manifestations of this is that I have known many men who if they see me with a woman, will tell me that they desperately want to meet her; but I'm sure that if they had not seen her with me they would not have had the slightest interest in the woman. This has happened many times, where I do arrange for them to meet the woman, they go out with her once, and then lose interest in her.

Girlfriend

Yes, I know what you mean, but what kind of problems are you talking about?

Man

Well shyness for one.

Girlfriend

But that's very common, what else?

Man

Well, impotence and or being non-orgastic for others, both of which afflict me.

Girlfriend

I don't know why I am telling you this, but I happen to be frigid; I guess that means that I am, what was that word you used, non-orgastic?

Man

But you're so beautiful.

Girlfriend

Can't a good looking woman be frigid?

Man

That surely is one of nature's biggest jokes.

Girlfriend

In fact, I was going to break off the relationship with the doctor tonight. This always happens; I have never had an orgasm with any man that I've ever dated and always end up breaking up with them. Also, he really wasn't a very nice person.

Man

Do you know why you are frigid or, as you put it, can't have an orgasm?

Girlfriend

Unfortunately, when I was a kid my mother used to say to me that a man could do things to a woman that were so bad that the woman would rather that the man had killed her.

Man

That's terrible!

Girlfriend

Yes, but your killing my date was worse.

Man

I don't understand how that happened. I can't believe I did such a thing. Pick up a pipe and hit him in the head.

Girlfriend

But it did happen.

Man

Do you remember saying to me that if I didn't kill you, you would never identify me?

Girlfriend

Yes, at that moment, I was afraid of you.

Man

But you are not afraid of me now?

Girlfriend

No. By the way, you keep saying that I am so beautiful. Did that have anything to do with your killing my date?

Man

Maybe, the idea of him having a woman that looks like you, rather than me having you, just galled me.

Girlfriend

I suppose that is flattering. But to get back to your therapy, you said that you and he argued for years over a woman. Why didn't you just quit the therapy?

Man

That's a good question. If you have never been to therapy it would be hard to explain.

Girlfriend

I have been to therapy, in fact, many therapies with different therapists, and it never seemed to help; but I have never had a problem quitting if the therapy didn't seem to be helping. What's it like to argue for years over something?

Man

The time goes by endlessly with the psychiatrist just whipping you verbally with flip remarks like "What do you think?" or "Why do you ask?" or "What's it all about?" and avoiding coming to grips with the incident where I supposedly froze up with the woman at work and he denying that it happened. You get angrier and angrier. Finally you begin to express the anger.

Girlfriend

Maybe that was the point of the therapy. Despite the fact that you killed somebody tonight, and I can't believe that I am saying this, but you do seem to be the kind of person that never gets angry, even when you should.

Man

You're not the first person to say that to me.

Girlfriend

So why do you feel that he was not doing his job; maybe his job was to get you so angry that you would express it?

Man

It was the way he ended the therapy.

Girlfriend

How was that?

Man

As I said, I was getting angrier and angrier and I started cursing and screaming. I started doing it when I was by myself. The problem was that I could not do it in the psychiatrist's office.

Girlfriend

You mean, you would curse and scream when you were alone in your apartment.

Man

Yes, and in my car too which is a better place than in the apartment. When I did it in my apartment, my neighbors could hear me and must have thought I was crazy. In the car nobody can hear you as long as the windows are closed, although once a co-worker drove by me and saw me gesticulating very vigorously by myself. He asked me about it at work the next day; I mollified him by saying that he caught me with a case of the "screamies." He was a "savvy" kind of guy and understood.

Girlfriend

Boy, the psychiatrist really did a number on you

Man

Gee, most people would say that I was so angry because I had transferred anger toward someone else, like my mother, onto him.

Girlfriend

Do you think that is a possibility?

Man

I guess it's possible. But I just felt that he was messing with me.

Girlfriend

You mean consciously.

Man

Oh maybe not consciously, but at some point he could have or should have checked out the situation with another analyst which I suggested. I don't think he ever did.

Girlfriend

Okay, go on.

Man

Eventually I was able to reach the point where one day I cursed and screamed at him in as loud and angry a voice in his office as I was doing when I was alone.

Girlfriend

How did he react?

Man

He said we would have to end if I was going to do this again. Unbelievably, I said, "Okay let's end." And I unilaterally picked an ending date about two weeks in the future; even though I had trepidations about letting the psychiatrist precipitate such an abrupt ending of the therapy.

Girlfriend

What happened when the day to end came?

Man

I expected him to say, "It was about time that I let him have it, and now we can really begin therapy." But all he said was that he had only been kidding and he said it in a very matter-of-fact way. I felt this was unconscionable, and I followed through on quitting.

Girlfriend

I think you did the right thing. You had to quit, if you could, after that.

Man

What was worse was that at the end of the appointed last session, he begged me to come one more time, which I did, and yet he still could not and did not say what I wanted him to say, so I continued on with the abrupt ending. I guess I must seem very unforgiving to you.

Girlfriend

Do you feel that you made a mistake in coming that one last time, that maybe you let him mess with you one more time?

Man

Somebody once said to me that I give everybody the benefit of the doubt and most of the time they don't deserve it.

Girlfriend

I'll say. You know maybe if you had ended when you said you would you might not have ended up killing him.

Man

Maybe so.

Girlfriend

On that extra day, did you at least scream at him when he didn't say what you wanted to hear?

Man

No!

Girlfriend

That might have discharged enough anger so that you might not have ended up killing him.

Man

What a pushover I was.

Girlfriend

I hope you didn't shake his hand when you left.

Man

I don't think so.

Girlfriend

I'll bet. The trouble with people like you is that you expect a psychiatrist to know what's happening during a therapy.

Man

Yes. I guess I do.

Girlfriend

You know—not to be too abrupt like your psychiatrist was in saying the therapy had to end if you didn't quiet down—here I am talking in a very matter-of-fact way with the man that killed my date tonight.

Man

Oh God. I still can't believe I did it.

Girlfriend

You know it just occurred to me that I am in serious trouble.

Man

You mean because you left the scene of the crime.

Girlfriend

Yes, but also because of your coming here and my letting you in.

Man

Why did you let me in?

Girlfriend

I am not sure, but you don't scare me; and, there is something about you that touches me.

Man

Do you like me?

Girlfriend

Let's not go into that. Let's get back to the reason why you killed my date. To a lot of people, the term countertransference sounds like so much "psychobabble."

Man

Yes, I know.

Girlfriend

Maybe there is another reason why you have problems with women.

Man

Well, like your childhood, my childhood was not perfect.

Girlfriend

Is anybody's?

Man

That's an interesting remark coming from a woman who might be frigid because of things her mother said to her. Are many women frigid?

Girlfriend

Probably more than you think: that's why so many women joke about faking having an orgasm. And why do you think there is such a high divorce rate?

Man

Are you saying that a lot of frigid women blame their frigidity on the choice of husband, and hope that with a different husband they will not be frigid?

Girlfriend

I'm sure that happens.

Man

Does that usually work?

Girlfriend

I have friends who were frigid with one man and not with another.

Man

But you have never found a man who you were not frigid with.

Girlfriend

There was one man where I was only partially frigid.

Man

What happened?

Girlfriend

He dumped me.

Man

Why would a man break off with a woman that looks like you?

Girlfriend

He said I was a bitch.

Man

Are you?

Girlfriend

Sometimes, without realizing it, but one of my therapists said that my bitchiness with that guy was the result of some "orgasm anxiety" that I was feeling, subconsciously, when I was with him.

Man

Not to try to psychoanalyze you, but tell me about your father.

Girlfriend

He was a very nice, gentle person. In fact he was sort of like you, but without the killing of my date.

Man

But he let your mother say things to you that she shouldn't have.

Girlfriend

A man has to work. He can't be around all day, watching his wife and child. Besides that, even when he was around, my mother still said terrible things, and he would mostly do nothing.

Man

Do you blame your father at all for your problem?

Girlfriend

I do, but what good does that do? He loved my mother; she "rang his bell" so to speak.

Man

But nobody's ever "rung your bell."

Girlfriend

With your sexual problems, I don't think you should be talking about having one's "bell rung."

Man

You can be bitchy.

Girlfriend

I'm sorry, but let's get back to you. You said your childhood was not perfect. Is it possible that your problems with women were caused by your less than perfect childhood?

Man

Of course!

Girlfriend

So maybe it wasn't the psychiatrist's fault.

Man

He didn't help.

Girlfriend

Were your parent's as less than perfect as mine?

Man

Maybe!

Girlfriend

What did they do that was so bad?

Man

Well for one, I had asthma as a teenager and when I would have an asthma attack, my mother would not call a doctor, at least not right away.

Girlfriend

Why not?

Man

When she was a little girl, she once had an earache and her mother wouldn't call the doctor until the neighbors forced her to, because she was screaming so loud.

Girlfriend

Was there a reason for that?

Man

My grandmother was a poor widow and did not want to spend the money.

Girlfriend

Did your mother not call a doctor when you had an asthma attack for the same reason?

Man

No, we were not that poor.

Girlfriend

So what happened when you had an asthma attack, did they go away by themselves?

Man

No, my mother would relent after a few days, and call the doctor. The doctor would come and give me an injection of adrenalin, which was the treatment in those days. But then my mother would say that the doctor just put water into my veins and that the asthma attack was only in my mind.

Girlfriend

By saying that your asthma attack was only in your mind, did your mother mean that the attack was imaginary, or that it was real but psychosomatically induced?

Man

She meant that it was imaginary, although she did see me gasping for breath. I guess she was in denial,—her own history overpowering her sense of reality.

Girlfriend

What about your father during these situations?

Man

I get the impression he was like your father, and let the mother rule the roost.

Girlfriend

Could these asthma attacks have anything to do with your sexual problems with women?

Man

Well I did develop having masochistic fantasies in order to get through long nights with full blown asthma attacks.

Girlfriend

How does that work?

Man

As my other psychiatrist indicated, because my mother would let me suffer, I wanted to hate her, but I couldn't. It seems that I had a choice: hate my mother or myself. I mean, who can hate their mother, so I ended up hating myself and this led to developing the masochistic fantasies. They seemed to help me get through the long sleepless nights gasping for breath when I had an asthma attack. Eventually, I outgrew the asthma, but the masochistic fantasies have stayed with me my whole life. I find them very embarrassing. This was exacerbated by a bad experience acting in a play with a director who used his position to brutalize me. This resulted in my cursing and screaming when by myself, like I did when I was in therapy. I blame this partly on my first psychiatrist, your date, the man I killed, who abruptly precipitated the ending of my therapy and left me not exactly expert in dealing with aggression. But I must admit that I knew I should have fought back against the director; for some reason I never got around to doing it.

Girlfriend

Yes, I think I understand. But more importantly, is there any chance that your problems with women are that, because of the way your mother treated you when you had asthma attacks, a part of you, deep down, hates her and this has spread, through transference, to unconsciously hating all women? I am a nurse, and I have a lot of experience with asthma. An asthma attack can be very painful. People die from asthma attacks. Your mother not calling the doctor right away when you were having an attack was very cruel, especially since an adrenalin injection by the doctor would have cured the attack immediately. It would make anybody very angry.

Man

You mean I'm guilty of disobeying the fifth commandment: "Honor thy father and mother."

Girlfriend

I don't know, maybe the word "honor" has more than one meaning, like possibly "respond in kind." Haven't you ever heard the expression "Honor an insult with an insult?"

Man

That's interesting, I never thought of that.

Girlfriend

Also, are you aware that most people misinterpret the biblical "an eye for an eye"? Most people feel that it means at least an eye for an eye, while I have heard it said by some savants that it means at most, or no more than, an eye for an eye.

Man

You seem to know a lot about religion.

Girlfriend

No, but I like to go to church. It is a good place to meet men who are okay.

Man

To get back to my mother, are you saying that I have transferred the negative part of my feelings toward my mother onto all women?

Girlfriend

Yes, and also, possibly that your anger toward my date was a transference of your repressed anger toward your mother onto him.

Man

But what about the mistakes he made?

Girlfriend

I accept the fact that he was not a good psychiatrist, but does that justify your killing him.

Man

Boy, you're tough? Are you finished?

Girlfriend

No, as far as there being no women in your life there could be other reasons. The fact that your mother wouldn't call the doctor when you had an asthma attack indicates that there were probably other things in your childhood that were problematic and would bring about a personality development that would make interactions with the opposite sex harder than necessary.

Man

You seem to know a lot about psychology.

Girlfriend

When you have psychological problems, you read up and learn about psychology. Although I never heard about countertransference until you told me about it.

Man

Okay to get back to my childhood, there were other things about my childhood which were problematic that could certainly be part of my problem with women.

Girlfriend

Can you give me an example?

Man

If I got hit by a kid and told my mother, she would say, "The next time you tell me a kid hit you, I'm going to hit you."

Girlfriend

Maybe she was trying to get you to fight back, although her reaction would certainly make it difficult for her to win the mother of the year award. How about giving me another example where her behavior was really unequivocally bad, besides the treatment you got when you had asthma attacks.

Man

Okay! Once when I visited my parents in Florida, I called up all my father's sisters who were living down there and made arrangements to visit them the next day, my mother hearing me do this. That night I woke up to find my mother shrieking bloody murder. My mother hated my father's sisters because they hated her for, crazy as it sounds, stealing my father away from them. This upset me so much that, in some curious way, I developed a phobia about flying on commercial airplanes. This phobia lasted for several years and almost cost me my job because I couldn't fly.

Girlfriend

That sounds bad. Maybe your parents or at least your mother were or was worse than the psychiatrist.

Man

Now wait a minute, parents can't help what they are, but a psychiatrist should be better.

Girlfriend

Okay, but what about your job causing your women problems? Some men are too busy or too absorbed with their work to give finding a woman the effort it deserves.

Man

That might be a problem in my case.

Girlfriend

What do you do for a living?

Man

I do scientific research involving the application of mathematics to crystallography.

Girlfriend

My experience with research scientists at the hospital, we have some since we are connected with a university, has taught me that research science is very demanding and some men, who do it, never find the wherewithal to go out and get a woman.

Man

Yes, I know. I always feel like a beginner, learning what I need to know to succeed as a researcher.

Girlfriend

You know, I just realized another reason why you had a problem with the psychiatrist. He felt threatened by you because of your research orientation; most men are going to feel inferior to you in the brains department.

Man

You mean because I am a research mathematician.

Girlfriend

Yes, also your manner, despite your having killed my date tonight, is very genial, which would make many men, oddly enough, be jealous of you and therefore feel threatened by you.

Man

I have noticed that a lot of men seem hostile to me when we first meet and I have done nothing to them. I always wondered why. Now I think I understand.

Girlfriend

So where are we? Do you really feel justified in blaming your first psychiatrist for your problems with women?

Man

The second psychiatrist thought so.

Girlfriend

But he might be wrong. Another thing, you know that you give an overall impression of being innocent and defenseless. This would cause a lot of people, especially unhappy people who don't have a lot going for them, like your first psychiatrist, to abuse you.

Man

I know that.

Girlfriend

You know, if your first psychiatrist was so bad, why didn't you just quit?

Man

It is not so easy for people like me who don't trust their feelings to just quit a therapy, and also, I had built up a lot of anger which I felt I had to resolve before I quit.

Girlfriend

Okay, but what about us, I can't believe I am saying this. Would you have approached me if you hadn't killed my date? Look what you did. You killed a man, followed me home and knocked on my door.

Man

I don't know. Did you notice me following you? It was quite a walk from the theater area to your apartment.

Girlfriend

Not really, I was too concerned about getting home.

Man

You know, if you had taken a cab, I might not have been able to follow you.

Girlfriend

I guess not.

Man

I'm glad you didn't take a cab.

Girlfriend

You know, if you are caught, you could go to jail for the rest of your life.

Man

But what about the fact that an impulse just came over me and it was not premeditated?

Girlfriend

How do you think the police, a judge, and a jury will feel about that?

Man

If you don't say anything about me to the police, I might never be caught.

Girlfriend

That could get me into trouble. Do you want to drag me down with you?

Man

No, I would want to get you into trouble.

Girlfriend

All right, I have an idea.

Man

What's that?

Girlfriend

If we get married, then I couldn't be asked to testify against you.

Man

That's right. Let's get married.

Girlfriend

Wait a minute. Slow down. Do you want to spend the night with me?

Man

Yes! But what if I can't "ring your bell" or do anything for that matter; it's been a long time since I've been with a woman?

Girlfriend

Let's find out.

Man

Why don't we just get married first?

Girlfriend

Not to seem too forward, but let us just go to bed tonight and check out the marriage thing tomorrow.

Man

Really!

Girlfriend

Yes, Really! Now stop talking and let's go to bed.

(They walk out together.)

Scene 2

At Rise:
Office with two detectives and a psychiatrist.

First Detective

Okay Doctor, tell us why you are here.

Psychiatrist

I read about the murder of that psychiatrist downtown and I think I know who did it.

Second Detective

How do you know this? Were you a witness to the crime?

Psychiatrist

No, but I think it was one of my old patients.

First Detective

Isn't any information that you can give us protected by doctor-patient privilege?

Psychiatrist

I thought that since a homicide is involved and also, since the patient never said anything about the killing to me, that doctor-patient privilege did not apply. Furthermore, my association with the patient ended before the killing of the psychiatrist.

First Detective

All right, tell us what you know.

Second Detective

Shouldn't we call the District Attorney's office and have an ADA here before the doctor starts talking?

First Detective

Let's see what the doctor has to say before calling an ADA. Go ahead, Doctor, talk to us.

Psychiatrist

As I said, I had a patient who prior to my treating him went to the psychiatrist who was killed.

First Detective

Don't many people go to several psychiatrists; and if one can't help them, they go to another?

Psychiatrist

Yes, that is certainly true.

Second Detective

So what's unusual about your patient and the psychiatrist who was killed?

Psychiatrist

The psychiatrist who was killed made a terrible mistake with the patient and I helped the patient to realize how much hatred he had deep down for the murdered psychiatrist because of the mistake.

First Detective

What was the mistake?

Psychiatrist

The doctor allowed what is known as countertransference to occur in the therapy, which caused the patient immeasurable harm.

Second Detective

Countertransference, what's that? I've heard of transference but never countertransference.

First Detective

Transference, isn't that where the patient supposedly falls in love with the psychiatrist?

Psychiatrist

Not exactly! Transference is where the patient develops feelings toward the psychiatrist, which first detective has characterized as falling in love, but they can be negative feelings like hatred, besides positive ones like love.

Second Detective

So what is countertransference?

Psychiatrist

Well, transference is where feelings flow from the patient to the psychiatrist; while countertransference, on the other hand, is where feelings flow in the opposite direction, from psychiatrist to patient. Also, in the case of psychiatrists dealing with patients, transference by the patient of feelings onto the psychiatrist is usually an integral part of a successful therapy, while countertransference usually causes problems.

First Detective

If countertransference usually causes problems in a therapy, why don't psychiatrists avoid it?

Psychiatrist

That seems to be almost impossible.

Second Detective

Why is that?

Psychiatrist

A psychiatrist is a living human being and feelings flowing toward the patient are almost unavoidable; and these feelings give rise to "countertransference."

First Detective

Shouldn't the training of psychiatrists include developing the ability to avoid countertransference?

Psychiatrist

You would hope, but it doesn't seem to work that way.

First Detective

So if countertransference is so common, and I presume that patients' killing their psychiatrists is not so common, why in this case did it lead to a killing?

Psychiatrist

Usually psychiatrists try to minimize the effects of countertransference or, hopefully the countertransference wasn't that bad; however, in this case, it was exceptionally bad and had a very deleterious effect on the patient.

Second Detective

What was the effect?

Psychiatrist

The therapy made it impossible for the patient to ever develop a good relationship with a woman.

First Detective

Countertransference can do that.

Psychiatrist

In my opinion, in this case, it did.

Second Detective

When you said in your opinion does that mean some psychiatrists would disagree with you?

Psychiatrist

Yes, especially the ones who are guilty of gross forms of countertransference with their own patients.

First Detective

I don't understand. You report on an ex-patient of yours who you think killed his previous psychiatrist, and yet you also seem to defend the patient almost to the point of excusing the killing.

Psychiatrist

I do have mixed feelings.

Second Detective

Can you explain why you have these mixed feelings?

Psychiatrist

On the one hand, murder is a crime. On the other hand, the behavior of the murdered psychiatrist toward the defendant was unconscionable. The psychiatrist indulged himself in such an egregious form of countertransference that once the defendant realized what the psychiatrist had done to him, it was almost understandable what happened.

First Detective

How long after the separation of the defendant from his old psychiatrist did the killing take place?

Psychiatrist

Almost ten years.

Second Detective

Why so long?

Psychiatrist

The defendant didn't realize what the psychiatrist had done to him for a long time

First Detective

Was the defendant going to you as a therapist at this time when he did realize it?

Psychiatrist

Yes.

Second Detective

You said before that you were instrumental in the defendant's realizing what the previous psychiatrist had done to him. Can you explain that?

Psychiatrist

Yes, I went over the details of the therapy of the defendant with the earlier psychiatrist, and both the defendant and I became aware of the malpractice of the previous psychiatrist in dealing with him.

First Detective

Then you might be partly responsible for the defendant killing his old psychiatrist.

Psychiatrist

In a way, yes, but I hope that I am not criminally responsible.

First Detective

No I don't think you are, but now we have to call for an ADA before we go on.

Second Detective

Okay, I'll make the call.

Scene 3

At Rise:
Office with the same two policemen as in the previous scene and the
girlfriend of the victim

First Detective

You were on a date with the victim the night he was killed.

Girlfriend

Yes.

Second Detective

(Showing the woman a picture of a man.) So tell us, is this the man
that killed your date?

Girlfriend

(After some nervous hesitation by the girlfriend.) No.

First Detective

Your body language tells us something different. People go to prison
because of body language that gets them convicted of something.

Girlfriend

I'm nervous.

Second Detective

I feel that you are not telling us the truth. Do you know what perjury is?

Girlfriend

Yes I know what perjury is. But I promised him that I would not
identify him if he didn't kill me.

First Detective

But that promise was made under duress, you are not obliged to keep that promise.

Girlfriend

But I swore on my life that I would not identify him.

First Detective

Let's talk about something else. Were you and the victim very close?

Girlfriend

Well, we were seeing each other, but I was beginning to feel that the relationship had to end.

Second Detective

Why is that?

Girlfriend

He wasn't a very nice man.

First Detective

In what way?

Girlfriend

He was very opinionated, wasn't very sympathetic for a psychiatrist, and I don't think he was a very good therapist.

Second Detective

Why do you say that?

Girlfriend

I have had a lot of therapy myself, and I could sense that he had too many of his own problems that could and would easily spill over onto his therapeutic practice.

First Detective

What happened the night he was killed?

Girlfriend

After leaving the theater that night, we walked toward his car.

Second Detective

The killing occurred a considerable distance from the theater district on an isolated street. What was the reason for that?

Girlfriend

Even though he was a doctor and made good money, he was cheap and didn't want to park his car in a lot where he would have to pay.

First Detective

So tell us what happened.

Girlfriend

This guy came up out of nowhere and had a pipe in his hand and before my date could do anything, he hit him on the head with the pipe.

Second Detective

Then what happened?

Girlfriend

He looked at me, raised the pipe to hit me, but I said, "Please don't kill me, I swear on my life that I'll never identify you."

First Detective

Then what happened.

Girlfriend

He just stared at me, and then he left.

Second Detective

Do you know what an accessory after the fact is?

Girlfriend

What do you mean?

First Detective

For being an accessory after the fact for murder, you could go to jail for 10 or more years. How old are you, thirty?

Girlfriend

I'm thirty-two.

Second Detective

You'd be about forty-two when you got out of jail. You might not be so good looking then.

First Detective

Again, is this the man who killed your date? (Showing her the picture again.)

Girlfriend

All right! Yes he is.

First Detective

Thank you.

Girlfriend

Can I go now?

First Detective

No. We don't believe that he just left after he killed the doctor. There's more. Isn't there?

Girlfriend

Yes, there is more.

First Detective

Can you please tell us?

Girlfriend

He followed me home, and knocked on my door.

Second Detective

What happened then?

Girlfriend

I let him in.

First Detective

You let him into your apartment. Weren't you afraid?

Girlfriend

No, if he was going to kill me, I thought that he would have done it when he killed my date.

Second Detective

Then what happened?

Girlfriend

We talked?

First Detective

Is that all?

Girlfriend

No, he spent the night with me.

Second Detective
What did you say?

Girlfriend
I said, "We spent the night together."

First Detective
Did he force you?

Girlfriend
No, it was consensual.

Second Detective
How did that come about?

Girlfriend
He kept saying how beautiful I was, and I felt sorry for him.

First Detective
Are you also saying that you like him?

Girlfriend
Yes, I do like him.

Second Detective
How do you explain that at one point during the night when the murder occurred you were so frightened that you said to the murderer that if he doesn't kill you, then you would never identify him, and then a little while later, you and he go to bed together without him forcing you?

Girlfriend
On taking a second look at him, I could tell that normally he was the kind of person that most people would consider harmless.

First Detective

But how could he be harmless and yet kill somebody?

Girlfriend

I guess everybody has their breaking point, even people we think of as harmless. I remember when I was a kid, there was this skinny kid with glasses that another kid, who was bigger, would pick on unmercifully, until one day the kid with glasses reached his limit and fought back. He did get the crap beat out of him, but he never got picked on again by the bigger kid.

Second Detective

(Speaking to the first detective.) I think we have reached a point where we should have an ADA present.

Girlfriend

And I am beginning to think that I have said too much. I think I should get myself a lawyer before I say anything more.

First Detective

Yes, you should. Do you know someone you can call?

Girlfriend

Yes I do.

Second Detective

Good! There are phones in the hall, you can make your call from there and I'll call the DA's office for an ADA to come over.

(The Girlfriend and the Second Detective leave.)

(Curtain to end Act I)

ACT II

Scene 1

At Rise:

Courtroom
Opening statements of prosecutor and defense.

Prosecutor

The defendant murdered a psychiatrist in cold blood by hitting him with a metal pipe. The defendant admits to the murder but the defense is claiming that there were mitigating circumstances and that the defendant acted under the impetus of a dissociative reaction, or in less technical terms, an "irresistible impulse." The reason given by the defense is that the defendant felt that the psychiatrist had hurt him very badly in the therapy that the defendant had with the psychiatrist. The state feels that there are not sufficient mitigating circumstances to justify such a brutal murder. If a patient thinks a doctor has made a mistake, then the patient has the right to bring a civil suit against the doctor. That's why doctors have malpractice insurance.

Defense

The defense feels that the psychiatrist who was murdered made a gross miscarriage of therapy by making a very serious mistake. The mistake was in allowing what is called countertransference to intrude itself into the therapy. Before explaining what countertransference is, it is necessary to explain the term "transference." Transference is the phenomenon in therapy where a patient transfers emotions, sometimes inappropriate ones, onto the psychiatrist. Therapy then, hopefully, helps the patient to resolve those emotions that are inappropriate and in doing so help the patient to solve some of his or her psychological problems. Countertransference, on the other hand, is where the psychiatrist's has inappropriate emotions toward the patient and these can have very deleterious effects on the therapy, which they did in the case of the defendant. In this case, the miscarriage was so great that the defendant was overpowered by an "irresistible impulse" when he saw the psychiatrist at a theater and followed him to a place where the murder took place. Therefore the defense asserts that the defendant is not guilty by reason of temporary insanity.

Scene 2

At Rise:

Courtroom
Prosecutor questioning psychiatrist for the state.

Prosecutor

As a practicing psychiatrist in this state for over twenty years, tell us what you think about the defendant.

Psychiatrist for the State

Before his therapy, the defendant was the kind of person, who finds it almost impossible to express anger. He was a walking victim, because of this inability to express anger which made him a "sitting duck" for all the people who want to take advantage of this weakness, and there are many. His psychiatrist sensed this. Hence the psychiatrist's job, among other things, was to make him so angry that he finally could be brought to the point of expressing anger. This was the only option. When a person goes to talk therapy, there are three things he can get: a friendly ear, good advice, and the benefits of a process. The first two need no explanation. The third one, which I called the process, involves transference. Unfortunately, transference can create an agonizing situation which it did in the case of the defendant. This led to the defendant reaching the point where he expressed his anger at the psychiatrist in a very explosive way which precipitated a rather abrupt ending to the therapy by the psychiatrist. This did not give the patient time to integrate into his personality a new found capability to express anger when necessary. But his psychiatrist was not fully aware of what was happening. I do not think he can be blamed for this, since he acted in a very human way of dealing with the incident of the defendant's explosive anger, albeit long overdue as a result of years of repressing it. Finally, as far as the defendant's problems with women, I do not think it can be blamed on his difficulties with his psychiatrist. The latter might have added to his difficulties with women but there seem to be possible other causes for it, like the defendant's anger toward his mother. In fact it is also possible that the defendant's anger toward the psychiatrist was primarily based on transference of his anger toward his mother onto the psychiatrist. To go one step further, however, even to blame the mother may be unjustified. Parents are never perfect, and to blame them for all the things that can go wrong when bringing up children is ridiculous. Parents give children life and that's a lot, because most everybody no matter how difficult their life is would rather be alive than not. How many people in prison, if given a choice between life imprisonment without the possibility of parole or the death penalty, would choose the latter? The answer is that most would choose the former. Hence, it is my considered opinion that the defendant killed his psychiatrist, not because of an "irresistible impulse" based on so-called countertransference, but that he did it out of ordinary, yet still controllable, anger toward the psychiatrist and is guilty of second degree murder.

Prosecutor

The prosecution rests.

Scene 3

At Rise:

Courtroom
Defense questions psychiatrist for the state.

Defense

I was struck in your previous testimony that people should be grateful for their parents giving them life. Is that all that one should expect from parents?

Psychiatrist for the State

There are limits, of course. I am not justifying child abuse by parents.

Defense

All right, let's go on. A psychiatrist for the defense will testify that the defendant killed his old psychiatrist when acting under "irresistible impulse." You and he disagree about this. Why should the court believe you and not the other psychiatrist?

Psychiatrist for the State

Because most talk therapists would agree with me.

Defense

Have you ever had any therapies where countertransference was a problem?

Psychiatrist for the State

I have had patients where there might have been countertransference but it never was a problem.

Defense

What about other psychiatrists, do some of them ever have patients where there were problems with countertransference?

Psychiatrist for the State

A few.

Defense

Any chance that the psychiatrists who agree with you, about "irresistible impulse" not being the cause of the defendant killing his old psychiatrist, had problems in therapies with countertransference and don't want to admit it?

Psychiatrist for the State

No.

Defense

How can you be so sure?

Psychiatrist for the State

I'm sure.

Defense

Is it possible that countertransference is the biggest problem in talk therapy?

Psychiatrist for the State

No.

Defense

It's not even a possibility?

Psychiatrist for the State

Maybe it's a small possibility. The biggest problem in talk therapy is how seriously disturbed a patient is.

Defense

Why is it that more and more psychiatrist are avoiding talk therapy and doing other forms of therapy like drug therapy?

Psychiatrist for the State

Because there seems to be no other way to help certain patients.

Defense

Don't they also make more money because they can treat two patients in an hour instead of one?

Psychiatrist for the State

Yes, that's true.

Defense

Does drug therapy cure patients or rather just make them more comfortable?

Psychiatrist for the State

Psychiatry can't cure all psychological problems.

Defense

So with some patients, drug therapy is just a palliative and does not lead to cure.

Psychiatrist for the State

You might say that.

Defense

We seem to have strayed a little from countertransference. I assert that the most common reason for lack of cure for patients who go for talk therapy is countertransference and that was the problem with the defendant and his old psychiatrist.

Psychiatrist for the State

I disagree.

Defense

Can you prove that I am wrong?

Psychiatrist for the State

No, I can't prove that, just like you can't prove that you're right.

Defense

We will have to let the jury decide that.

Psychiatrist for the State

Yes.

Defense

I have no more questions for this witness.

Scene 4

At Rise:

Courtroom
Defense is examining the psychiatrist who reported the defendant to the police.

Defense

Doctor, tell us what you think happened between the defendant and his psychiatrist.

Psychiatrist

The defendant acted under, in psychological terms, a dissociative reaction, or in less technical language, an "irresistible impulse" when he killed his psychiatrist and should be judged not guilty by reason of temporary insanity?

Defense

Is the defendant insane?

Psychiatrist

No, he committed the killing when he was only temporarily insane as a result of being so mistreated by the psychiatrist.

Defense

What could the previous psychiatrist have done that was so bad as to make the defendant act under an "irresistible impulse" and kill him?

Psychiatrist

The previous psychiatrist indulged himself in what is known as "countertransference" with the defendant as you indicated in your opening. This went on for several years.

Defense

Can you give us a layman's explanation of the term "countertransference"?

Psychiatrist

In layman's terms it means that the psychiatrist own problems spill over onto a therapy.

Defense

What was the upshot of this?

Psychiatrist

After the therapy with the previous psychiatrist, the defendant was never able to establish a good sexual relationship with a woman who appealed to him.

Defense

Are you saying that the cause of this problem with women was countertransference on the part of the previous psychiatrist toward the defendant during his therapy?

Psychiatrist

Yes.

Defense

Are you sure?

Psychiatrist

Yes.

Defense

How can you be so sure?

Psychiatrist

I spent a lot of time with the defendant and heard what his previous psychiatrist did to him.

Defense

Can you describe what the previous psychiatrist did to the defendant?

Psychiatrist

In technical terms the old psychiatrist exacerbated the Oedipus complex of the defendant by playing the role of a disapproving father making it impossible for the defendant to establish a satisfactory relationship with a mother surrogate, namely another woman.

Defense

Isn't the Oedipus complex derived from an ancient Greek play where a son kills his father and marries his mother?

Psychiatrist

Yes, but in modern parlance, a son doesn't kill his father, just maybe resents him, and goes out and finds a suitable woman not his mother, but a substitute for her. In the defendants case it became impossible to get a suitable woman because of the mistake made by the psychiatrist.

Defense

Can you explain in detail how this came about?

Psychiatrist

An incident came up where a woman that the defendant liked seemed to give him a possible opening to make contact with her. The patient, as he described it to me, froze and didn't try to take advantage of the situation. Also, he didn't realize what he was doing at the time (by repressing what had happened). He reported the incident to the psychiatrist who said nothing at the time. Then later when the patient realized (or in technical terms stopped repressing) what had happened, he brought up the issue of what he had done and why he had not responded. This was a recurrent problem with him and he thought this would be a good example of his problem to use to try to change his behavior in these situations. The psychiatrist refused to discuss it saying that nothing had happened. The patient, and I think rightfully so, then told the psychiatrist that the psychiatrist was saying the incident never occurred or, in other words, that nothing had happened because the psychiatrist (subconsciously) felt guilty about not immediately making the patient aware of what he, the patient, had done and exploring the situation with the patient. This then, unbelievably, led to years of arguing about this one incident.

Defense

How is this countertransference?

Psychiatrist

For one reason or another, the psychiatrist could not admit that he had made a mistake and because of this, there was a feeling of anger of the psychiatrist toward the patient. This then, in the curious way that the subconscious works, because there was a woman involved, became a replay of the primal oedipal situation where the psychiatrist, as I said before, becomes the disapproving father preventing the son from getting a woman who would be a substitute for the mother. This led to the patient having greater and greater problems with women which eventually led to women becoming off limits to him.

Defense

But don't a lot of men have problems with women, especially if the women appeal to them?

Psychiatrist

Yes, but not as bad as the defendant's problem; and, if they do, then they sometimes go to a psychiatrist for help.

Defense

And if they don't go to a psychiatrist or get help some other way, what happens?

Psychiatrist

They don't have good relationships with women, unless they are lucky somehow.

Defense

Does that mean, that once the defendant thought (in his subconscious) that the psychiatrist had exacerbated his problems with women to the point where he felt that he probably could never get a woman, that when he, one day accidentally crossed paths with the psychiatrist, killed him under the impetus of an "irresistible impulse"?

Psychiatrist

Yes. And it didn't help that when the defendant crossed paths with the psychiatrist, the psychiatrist was with a very beautiful woman, the kind of woman the defendant would have liked to get for himself. I guess he felt subconsciously that if he could not have a woman, why should his old psychiatrist be able to have one, and such a beautiful one at that

Defense

Why do you think the defendant didn't kill the woman the psychiatrist was with? Without her eyewitness identification, there would be no direct evidence against him.

Psychiatrist

He is basically not a violent man and couldn't bring himself to kill her, even at the risk of getting caught; and, by the way, as far as I am concerned, this proves that when he killed the psychiatrist he was acting under an "irresistible impulse."

Defense

(Looking at audience.) Some or all of you on the jury are wondering if the woman, who the psychiatrist was with the night he was killed, will be called as a witness. This will not happen, since the defendant has admitted to killing the psychiatrist and therefore she is not needed for these proceedings. Furthermore, as per the Judge's instructions, for reasons that cannot be revealed, nothing more will be said about the woman by either myself or the prosecutor.

Psychiatrist

I wondered why the psychiatrist's girlfriend was not on the witness list for either the prosecution or the defense.

Defense

That is not for you to concern yourself with, Doctor.

Psychiatrist

I think I understand.

Defense

I have no more questions for this witness.

Scene 5

At Rise:

Courtroom
Prosecutor is questioning psychiatrist who reported the defendant to the police.

Prosecutor
Even though you were the one who reported the defendant to the police, you seem to have a great sympathy for him. You have said that you believe his killing his old psychiatrist was the result of an "irresistible impulse"?

Psychiatrist
Yes I did.

Prosecutor
Then why did you essentially turn him in? He might never have been caught if you hadn't reported him.

Psychiatrist
I felt obliged to.

Prosecutor
And you don't feel you violated doctor-patient privilege?

Psychiatrist
No.

Prosecutor
What exactly did the victim do that was so bad that it resulted in his being killed?

Psychiatrist

He indulged himself in a particularly destructive form, as already indicated to the court, of what is called countertransference in therapy and it hurt the defendant very much.

Prosecutor

If this is true, then why was there such a long time between the end of the defendant's therapy with the first psychiatrist and the defendant's killing him?

Psychiatrist

He didn't realize how much his therapy had hurt him until he came to me as a patient.

Prosecutor

I once saw a television show, where a therapist brainwashes a patient into believing that her father had sexually molested her when she was a child, when in reality he hadn't?

Psychiatrist

I saw that show. It was excellent with a great actress playing the therapist.

Prosecutor

Any chance you brainwashed the defendant into believing that his previous psychiatrist had been bad, which resulted in his being killed, when he wasn't really that bad.

Psychiatrist

In my opinion, no chance whatsoever.

Prosecutor

How can you be so sure?

Psychiatrist

Because I have devoted the majority of my career to dealing with patients who have had unsuccessful talk therapies, like the therapy that the defendant had with the psychiatrist he killed, and who come to me to repair the damage.

Prosecutor

Why do you do this?

Psychiatrist

Because it is needed. Some people, who go to talk therapy psychiatrists, come out of it not only not helped but hurt very much.

Prosecutor

Do you feel this way about most medical specialties?

Psychiatrist

No. Most medical specialists are very effective. The practice of talk therapy psychiatry or psychoanalysis or psychotherapy is one of the exceptions.

Prosecutor

And why is this?

Psychiatrist

Psychological problems are very difficult to treat; and, also many people who go into the practice of the kind of therapy that is called talk therapy sometimes have problems of their own, which spill over into the therapy, causing the ugly specter of countertransference to rear its ugly head as it did with the defendant.

Prosecutor

Don't therapists have to have a training therapy to avoid problems like this from happening?

Psychiatrist

Not all therapists have a training therapy as part of their training; and even if they do, it might not help for various reasons.

Prosecutor

You have described countertransference when you were questioned by the defense attorney; and it is not necessary to repeat any of your responses. But tell us how a patient feels when he is being victimized by countertransference.

Psychiatrist

He feels that his time and money are being wasted by the psychiatrist endlessly avoiding what the patient feels is important, and a lot of anger is generated which the patient is unable to express. In the case of the defendant, an incident occurred where he froze up with a woman he was interested in and, when he realized what he had done, he wanted to explore why. The psychiatrist refused to explore the situation saying that nothing had happened. All this has already been indicated.

Prosecutor

Why would the psychiatrist do this?

Psychiatrist

Because of countertransference, which manifested itself in that he couldn't admit that he had made a mistake, which led to the psychiatrist becoming angry at the defendant.

Prosecutor

It doesn't sound like enough justification for the defendant killing the psychiatrist.

Psychiatrist

It isn't, but the defendant felt that this incident characterized his problems with women and hoped that by exploring this situation with his psychiatrist he would find out why he had problems with women and maybe get over them. He felt that the psychiatrist failed him.

Prosecutor

Could it have been that the woman hadn't really given the defendant an opportunity to respond to her?

Psychiatrist

Of course, but checking out the situation, instead of freezing up and not responding, would have resolved that. I mean most men when they see a woman who appeals to them are capable of wishful thinking and imagining the woman is showing interest in them even if she really isn't. And if they approach her and she doesn't respond, they back off.

Prosecutor

All right, so the psychiatrist didn't help, but why kill him? Just because a psychiatrist is not effective or is even harmful to a patient, does that mean he deserves to die?

Psychiatrist

I didn't say he deserved to die.

Prosecutor

But you are saying that the psychiatrist who was killed was responsible for the defendant having problems responding successfully to a woman.

Psychiatrist

Yes.

Prosecutor

Could a psychiatrist have had that much effect on a patient?

Psychiatrist

In my considered opinion, based on many years of experience, absolutely.

Prosecutor

And you feel that this justifies the anger the defendant felt toward the psychiatrist.

Psychiatrist

Yes, the psychiatrist endlessly avoided trying to resolve the mistake the defendant thought he had made. Furthermore, the defendant's life was on hold, waiting to get help from the psychiatrist. Do you know that while the defendant was going to the psychiatrist, more than half of his take home pay went to pay for it? This went on for years.

Prosecutor

So what happened eventually?

Psychiatrist

After a while the defendant would come home from therapy and start cursing and screaming in his apartment. He told me that he once went out with a woman that lived on his floor in his apartment building, and when he asked her if anybody on the floor could hear him cursing and screaming, she said, "Yes, you are known as the man that screams in the night." It was amazing that she went out with him.

Prosecutor

Why didn't the defendant curse and scream in the doctor's office?

Psychiatrist

It is not so easy to do that in the psychiatrist's office, especially if the psychiatrist objects to it. For example, this psychiatrist in warm weather would leave his office window open, instead of using the air conditioning, and say that people in nearby offices would complain if the defendant raised his voice. Furthermore, if the patient was the kind of person that could curse and scream easily in a psychiatrist's office, he probably would be the kind of person that would not need therapy.

Prosecutor

If a patient thinks the therapist has made a mistake, why is it necessary for the patient to raise his voice?

Psychiatrist

Because, not only do we communicate by what we say but also, and this is very important, by how we say it. If a person is angry and doesn't use an angry tone of voice, some people will not realize that they have made him angry.

Prosecutor

All right, go on.

Psychiatrist

Finally by gradually building up to it, the defendant one day was finally able to bring himself to curse and scream at the psychiatrist in his office with the same intensity he had been doing when by himself.

Prosecutor

What happened then?

Psychiatrist

The psychiatrist, on that day, said that if the defendant was going to curse and scream like that in the office, the therapy would have to end. The defendant had the good sense to say, at least as far as I am concerned, okay let the therapy end and picked, unilaterally, a time—a couple of weeks in the future—when it should happen. When the time to end came the psychiatrist said, in a matter-of-fact way, that he had only been kidding. But the defendant followed through on ending the therapy, feeling that the therapy was going nowhere and also that it was not necessary to continue. I agree with this.

Prosecutor

So the defendant ended with that psychiatrist and eventually came to you.

Psychiatrist

Yes, and I made him realize what had been done to him as far as trying to establish a good relationship with a woman. The psychiatrist had, because of the oedipal complications, intensified the defendant's hesitation and avoidance reactions to women. So one day when he spotted the psychiatrist out with a woman, he was so overcome by an "irresistible impulse" that he followed the couple to their car which was in an isolated place and picked up a pipe, laying in the street, and hit the psychiatrist, killing him.

Prosecutor

So in a sense you are partly responsible for the murder of the psychiatrist.

Psychiatrist

You could say that.

Prosecutor

And maybe that's why you reported the defendant to the police.

Psychiatrist

You are probably right, but I still feel that the crime was based on an "irresistible impulse" and should not be considered murder.

Prosecutor

Even if what you say is correct and the malpractice of the psychiatrist caused it to become impossible for the defendant to have a decent relationship with a woman, is that an excuse for killing him?

Psychiatrist

No, but would you want to live without good relationships with women?

Prosecutor

They're important but not necessary.

Psychiatrist

I think most men would disagree with you.

Prosecutor

Do you feel that the psychiatrist did what he did out of malice and not just incompetence?

Psychiatrist

Yes, the defendant asked, several times, for the old psychiatrist to check out the problem between them with another psychiatrist, and the old psychiatrist never did.

Prosecutor

And this was wrong?

Psychiatrist

Yes.

Prosecutor

Would every psychiatrist agree that the old psychiatrist should have checked out this situation with the defendant with another psychiatrist?

Psychiatrist

No, some psychiatrists would just consider that the defendant was indulging in what is called "negative transference"; namely, transference of negative feelings resulting from an earlier troubled childhood relationship onto the psychiatrist. This would more likely be the case if the psychiatrist had problems with countertransference in his practice.

Prosecutor

Well, I don't want to let this be a battle between experts; I want the jury, using common sense, to decide. But I have trouble believing that the psychiatrist could have such a strong effect on the defendant as to make it impossible for him to go out and get a woman. Why didn't the defendant just quit therapy?

Psychiatrist

You don't realize the power of the connection that develops between a patient and the therapist when in a psychoanalytic talk therapy relationship. If the therapist is good this might bring about a cure or improvement. But if the therapist is not good, this could result in what the patient went through. As far as quitting is concerned the patient is locked in. This is because of the strong emotions produced in therapy like an accumulation of unexpressed anger or one might say, an "anger debt," and the fact that the patient has invested so much time and money in the therapy. Freud called this situation, Analysis-Terminable-Interminable. Think of a bad therapy situation as a bad marriage. It sometimes is, for some people, as difficult to get out of a bad therapy as it is to get out of a bad marriage.

Prosecutor

But no matter how bad the situation is, does it excuse murder. Consider a situation where a surgeon makes a mistake which leaves a patient paralyzed, would the patient be justified in killing the surgeon, if he could.

Psychiatrist

It doesn't excuse murder and the answer to your question is no.

Prosecutor

What's different?

Psychiatrist

The surgeon might have made a momentary mistake that was not correctable, once it was made. The psychiatrist who was killed had many opportunities to correct what he was doing wrong.

Prosecutor

That's your opinion, which I, and probably a lot of psychiatrists, disagree with

Psychiatrist

Okay.

Prosecutor

Is it possible that the defendant's problem with women is based on something else, like possibly that he is gay?

Psychiatrist

No, he is not gay. I can tell if a person is gay when I get to know them as well as I did the patient.

Prosecutor

Are you gay?

Psychiatrist

No, are you?

Prosecutor

If you don't mind, I'll ask the questions; let's go on. What about the fact that the defendant is a mathematician and I have heard it said that mathematicians are notorious for having problems with women? Supposedly, the greatest mathematician of all time, Isaac Newton, had lots of difficulties with women. In fact, isn't there a saying that "mathematics is a jealous mistress?"

Psychiatrist

Not all mathematicians have problems with women. The almost as great mathematician as Newton, Gauss, wrote beautiful love letters to the woman who eventually became his wife.

Prosecutor

All right, what about the fact that the defendant was the kind of person who could not express anger in his therapy or in life in general, until he finally was forced to do so because he got so angry at the psychiatrist's countertransference and without the countertransference this would never have happened?

Psychiatrist

Even if that were true the countertransference still could have intensified the defendant's problems with women, and the ability to express anger could have been developed in another way. Furthermore, because of the abrupt ending of the therapy, precipitated by the psychiatrist, the patient never really learned how to deal with and express anger appropriately; and this could have led to the defendants killing the psychiatrist.

Prosecutor

But, appropriately or not, the defendant did learn how to express anger and isn't it considered a fact by most psychiatrists that the inability to express anger at all can be a very serious problem, causing physical problems like asthma, migraine headaches and ulcers among others, and also things like automobile accidents. My experience has been that when an automobile accident is a result of alcohol, there was usually some repressed anger which brought about the drinking.

Psychiatrist

But that still doesn't justify the old psychiatrist's behavior.

Prosecutor

That's for the jury to decide. I have no more questions for this witness.

Scene 6

At Rise:

Courtroom
Defense Attorney is questioning defendant.

Defense

Tell us about the night the incident with your old psychiatrist occurred.

Defendant

I went to a play in a downtown theater one night and on leaving the theater after the performance had ended, I saw my old psychiatrist with a woman. The woman was very beautiful. For some unfathomable reason, I started following them. We got to an isolated street where it was just them and me. They didn't seem to notice that I was following them. I seem to go into a daze. I saw a metal pipe on the ground and I picked it up and got near to them. When I got very close the doctor turned around and noticed me, and without realizing what I was doing, I hit him with the pipe.

Defense

Then what happened.

Defendant

I left but stayed close enough so I could follow the woman home. When she got home, I knocked on her door.

Defense

Why did you do that?

Defendant

I don't know why; it just seemed to happen.

Defense

Okay, then what happened?

Defendant

She let me in.

Defense

And?

Defendant

We talked.

Defense

Anything else?

Defendant

We ended up going to bed together.

Defense

Did you force her?

Defendant

No, it was consensual.

Defense

Do you realize that if you also had killed her, you might have not been caught?

Defendant

Yes, but I killed the doctor because of an "irresistible impulse" and would never have killed the woman.

Defense

Why was there such a long time period between your ending your treatment with the doctor and your killing him?

Defendant

It took me a long time before I realized what he had done to me.

Defense

What made you realize what he had done to you?

Defendant

I went to a second psychiatrist, who has already testified about this for the court, who made me realize what had happened to me in my previous therapy.

Defense

You mean that you were not angry at the first psychiatrist till you went to the second psychiatrist.

Defendant

Oh, I was angry all right, but it was sort of unfocused anger; I use to curse and scream by myself without really knowing why.

Defense

Where would you do this cursing and screaming?

Defendant

Mostly in my car when driving. Although sometimes in my apartment. I tried not to do the latter for fear that people could hear me and think I was crazy.

Defense

You mean you would spontaneously start cursing and screaming by yourself.

Defendant

Yes, in fact that's why, although after a long time, I started going to the second psychiatrist.

Defense

And it was in the second therapy that you became fully cognizant of what had happened to you in your first therapy?

Defendant

Yes.

Defense

And you think that your realization of your first psychiatrist's malpractice is what set you off when you saw him at the theater and led to your killing him.

Defendant

Yes.

Defense

Were you aware of what you were doing when you hit the psychiatrist with the pipe?

Defendant

No. It was a purely impulsive act. I just went blank and hit him with the pipe. I am really sorry. If I had just not blanked out, I would not have done it. I can't believe I did such a terrible thing.

Defense

The defense rests.

Scene 7

At Rise:

Courtroom
Prosecutor questioning defendant.

Prosecutor

So you want this court to believe that you are not criminally responsible for killing your old psychiatrist?

Defendant

Yes, I just lost it.

Prosecutor

Would you have killed the psychiatrist if you hadn't gone to the second psychiatrist and through him learned of what your first psychiatrist supposedly did to you?

Defendant

I don't know.

Prosecutor

Were his actions as a therapist, criminal?

Defendant

I think so.

Prosecutor

If a doctor makes a mistake that is called malpractice, should criminal charges be brought against him?

Defendant

No, unless it can be shown that the mistake was correctable and the doctor refused to correct it, or, if not correctible, that the mistake was easily avoidable.

Prosecutor

If an officer in the military makes a mistake in a battle and it causes several men to die unnecessarily, is that criminal?

Defendant

I don't know. But during the Vietnam War, didn't officers get "fragged" if they made a mistake that cost unnecessary lives?

Prosecutor

Was Robert E. Lee doing something criminal when he ordered Pickett's charge on the third day at Gettysburg? Think of all the confederate soldiers that were killed, and if not killed, mutilated losing arms and legs in that charge.

Defendant

I read that the southern commander in the field there, James Longstreet, could not bring himself to give the verbal order to charge but that he just nodded his head when asked if the charge should begin; and, also, that Pickett himself after the charge never spoke to Lee again.

Prosecutor

Do you think those confederates who survived Pickett's charge, but lost parts of their bodies and maybe could never get a woman because of it, hated Lee?

Defendant

I don't know.

Prosecutor

Lee was a great general because he pushed to the limit and Pickett's charge was the one time he went too far. If he had never gone too far that one time, it probably would have meant that he was not pushing to the limit in battles like he did when he gambled and won mightily at Chancellorsville, and he would have been just another mediocre general.

Defendant

Is this a civil war history lesson?

Prosecutor

Could it be that you were the only patient of your first psychiatrist that he had countertransference problems with?

Defendant

Is that an excuse for his behavior?

Prosecutor

Possibly, and don't forget that Lee's soldiers were for the most part draftees, while you of your own free will chose to go to a psychiatrist. Why did you go?

Defendant

I had a problem with a woman.

Prosecutor

What was the problem?

Defendant

We were going together and had reached the point where we had to get married or break up and I couldn't do either.

Prosecutor

You mean you lacked the courage to do one or the other.

Defendant

All right, yes.

Prosecutor

Could it be that your difficulties with your psychiatrist were appropriate punishment for your not having the courage to bring a relationship to some sort of closure on your own?

Defendant

That's sort of cynical.

Prosecutor

Tell the court again what your first psychiatrist did to you that was so bad?

Defendant

He kept jerking me around endlessly when I would bring up some incident which I thought was important to explore, where I felt he had made a mistake. Exploring this incident might have been key to my having a successful therapy. I kept trying to corner him to face up to what he had done but he kept twisting and turning to avoid the issue and so we never could resolve it.

Prosecutor

You know the average person would have just given up and quit going to that psychiatrist. I am not a therapist but I wonder if your problem was that you had been looking for and finally found a thing you felt was a mistake of your therapist's and then latched onto that like a bulldog and never let go.

Defendant

But it was a mistake.

Prosecutor

Is it easy for you to admit your mistakes?

Defendant

No, but I am not a therapist. And I told him he was making a mistake and should check it out with another therapist.

Prosecutor

How do you know he didn't?

Defendant

The second psychiatrist said the first psychiatrist would have told me if he had.

Prosecutor

Oh really, I don't believe that. Not many people can openly admit they made a mistake.

Defendant

Okay, you disagree with what the second therapist says.

Prosecutor

Not to rehash what has already been said, what was the final result of what the first psychiatrist did to you?

Defendant

It seems he made it impossible for me ever to have a good relationship with a woman.

Prosecutor

Even if that were true, did he deserve to die for that?

Defendant

No, but I killed him because of "irresistible impulse", not because he deserved to die.

Prosecutor

Supposedly, you learned from your second psychiatrist that the first psychiatrist was responsible for your not being able to have relationships with women. Do you think that all psychiatrists would agree with him?

Defendant

I don't know.

Prosecutor

Couldn't there be another reason why you don't have relationships with women?

Defendant

What other reason?

Prosecutor

That you could never commit to a relationship.

Defendant

Well, I do have problems with commitment.

Prosecutor

I'm sure you do. How many books do you have that you have never read but are hoping to read someday?

Defendant

What does that have to do with problems with commitment?

Prosecutor

You see a book that interests you and you buy it, bring it home and then put it on a shelf and never get around to reading it. Don't you see how that ties in with your commitment problems?

Defendant

Couldn't it be that I just like to collect books?

Prosecutor

I guess you are going to read all those books when you grow up.

Defendant

Sometimes you get a lot out of a book by just browsing in it.

Prosecutor

Let's talk about women. Do many women throw themselves at you?

Defendant

Some.

Prosecutor

I get the impression you don't take advantage of most of these situations.

Defendant

That's true.

Prosecutor

Do you know why?

Defendant

They either aren't my type; or, if they are my type, I couldn't bring myself to respond appropriately when I had the opportunity.

Prosecutor

Why dont you respond appropriately?

Defendant

I don't know. I guess I blame that on my first psychiatrist and the countertransference.

Prosecutor

So you think not responding appropriately was not your fault?

Defendant

Yes.

Prosecutor

Have you not only not responded but ran away from some women, even some that you liked?

Defendant

Yes, unfortunately.

Prosecutor

How do you feel about that?

Defendant

Terrible.

Prosecutor

But it never was your fault, only your psychiatrist's?

Defendant

All right maybe it was partly my fault. I wish I hadn't run away from some of them.

Prosecutor

How about the fact that being a mathematician is another reason you do not have relationships with women? When you were young, you focused on learning mathematics instead of chasing women like most young men do. We have already heard about Isaac Newton and his problems with women.

Defendant

I did spend some crucial years just studying and maybe because of that developed some bad habits, which I rather not discuss, but I am certainly not in the class of Isaac Newton.

Prosecutor

Why did you study mathematics?

Defendant

Because I felt that mathematics explains the ultimate secrets of the universe.

Prosecutor

And you wanted the power and security of knowing the ultimate secrets of the universe.

Defendant

You might say so.

Prosecutor

But that wasn't enough for you. You wanted women also, even though it is possible that the real progress of science is usually paid for by the essential celibacy of mathematicians. I am going to let you in on something that might surprise you. I majored in mathematics in college and when I was near graduation I had a choice: to go on to graduate school in mathematics with all its precise perfection, but with no women, or go on to law school, and the loose slipperiness of words, and enjoy the pleasures of women. As you can see I chose the latter.

Defendant

There are happily married mathematicians.

Prosecutor

Are you sure?

Defendant

Well I haven't taken a survey.

Prosecutor

What about courage? Could it be that mathematicians with their need to understand the ultimate secrets of the universe, and you especially, find it difficult to do things just because they feel like doing it, where courage is required, but always have to be absolutely sure before they do anything?

Defendant

Yes I don't trust my feelings and there were times in my life when I wish I had had more courage.

Prosecutor

But you killed somebody; that took courage, although a sick and socially unacceptable kind.

Defendant

That was not me acting normally, but me acting under "irresistible impulse."

Prosecutor

Oh really; let's get to the bottom of all this: do you feel that there was any justification for killing your first psychiatrist?

Defendant

I don't say that it was justified; it was a momentary impulse. But for years the psychiatrist just toyed with me, wasting my time and money, refusing to deal with an issue that I thought got to the heart of my problems. It went on and on until I got so mad that I started cursing and screaming when by myself.

Prosecutor

So what did you do then?

Defendant

The therapy ended after I finally expressed my full anger in the psychiatrist's office, and after a long while, I started going to another psychiatrist who made me realize what had gone wrong with the first therapy, namely what is called, as has already been indicated, countertransference on the part of the first psychiatrist.

Prosecutor

Do you know that most people, and some doctors, even, have never heard of the word "countertransference"?

Defendant

Yes, I didn't know the word until I began reading up on therapy to find out what was going wrong with mine.

Prosecutor

Couldn't it be that what your first psychiatrist did to you was just normal human interaction where if somebody is too much of a victim type, like I think you are, he gets victimized until he learns how not to be a victim anymore, if he ever does? Your first psychiatrist did exactly what he was supposed to do. He kept pushing you around until you finally learned how to express the normal human emotion of fighting back. You probably got more out of therapy than most people. Your problems with women have little to do with supposed mistakes that were made by your old psychiatrist. You killed him because you blamed him, and unjustly I might add, for your problems with women.

Defendant

That's not true.

Prosecutor

We'll have to see how the jury feels about that. I am finished with the defendant.

Scene 8

At Rise:

Courtroom
Defense and prosecution summaries.

Defense

Killing somebody is never good. Even in war it puts a heavy burden on some soldiers. The public is not in agreement about the death penalty for criminals or euthanasia for terminally ill people in pain. Nevertheless the dissociative reaction, or "irresistible impulse," in this case, has been allowed in the court as a mitigating cause for killing someone in certain circumstances. The case before you is one of those circumstances. Even if the countertransference did yield a benefit to the defendant of bringing about the acquiring of the ability to express anger, there are other ways of developing this ability, but the countertransference resulted in the defendant not being able to have good relationships with women. Hence the price paid by the defendant of having to live without women was unnecessarily high and resulted in the "irresistible impulse" of killing his old psychiatrist. Therefore, members of the jury, if you accept this premise in any way, there is reasonable doubt, and your verdict should be not guilty by reason of temporary insanity.

Prosecutor

It is true that "irresistible impulse" in certain cases has been used as an excuse for killing somebody. I do not think that it applies in this case. Doctors make mistakes all the time. Even if the psychiatrist who was killed was responsible for the defendant's problems with women because of so-called "countertransference," that does not justify his being killed. If a doctor's mistake is egregious enough then a malpractice suit can be initiated. But did the psychiatrist really make a mistake. The defendant is the kind of person that gets abused, because he invites it, probably unknowingly. Most people sense this and try not to abuse him, but some people cannot control themselves, because of their own needs. If they meet a person like the defendant they cannot resist abusing him. The psychiatrist sensed this weakness in the defendant and forced him to express real anger for the first time in his life. Since most therapists agree that the ability to express anger is critical to overcome this weakness of letting people abuse one, the therapy worked. In other words the defendant was cured by what his old psychiatrist did. Hence he, the defendant, had no justification to kill his old psychiatrist and therefore "irresistible impulse" was not in play just ordinary, controllable anger, which the defendant did not control. Therefore you, the jury, should bring in a verdict of guilty of murder in the second degree.

Edwards Brothers Malloy
Thorofare, NJ USA
September 17, 2012